GEARED FOR GROWTH BIBLE STUDIES
GOD'S HEART MY HEART
WHAT THE BIBLE SAYS ABOUT WORLD MISSION

BIBLE STUDIES TO IMPACT THE LIVES OF ORDINARY PEOPLE

Christian Focus Publications

The Word Worldwide

Written by Ivan Bowden
Additional notes by various WEC missionaries

Christian Focus Publications
publishes books for all ages

Our mission statement –

STAYING FAITHFUL

In dependence upon God we seek to help make His infallible word, the Bible, relevant. Our aim is to ensure that the Lord Jesus Christ is presented as the only hope to obtain forgiveness of sin, live a useful life and look forward to heaven with Him.

REACHING OUT

Christ's last command requires us to reach out to our world with His gospel. We seek to help fulfill that by publishing books that point people towards Jesus and help them develop a Christ-like maturity. We aim to equip all levels of readers for life, work, ministry and mission.

Books in our adult range are published in three imprints.

Christian Focus contains popular works including biographies, commentaries, basic doctrine, and Christian living. Our children's books are also published in this imprint.

Mentor focuses on books written at a level suitable for Bible College and seminary students, pastors, and other serious readers; the imprint includes commentaries, doctrinal studies, examination of current issues, and church history.

Christian Heritage contains classic writings from the past.

For details of our titles visit us on our website
www.christianfocus.com

ISBN 1-85792-892-X

Copyright © WEC International

Published in 2003 by
Christian Focus Publications, Geanies House,
Fearn, Ross-shire, IV20 1TW, Scotland
and
WEC International, Bulstrode, Oxford Road,
Gerrards Cross, Bucks, SL9 8SZ

Cover design by Alister MacInnes

Printed and bound by J W Arrowsmith, Bristol

CONTENTS

PREFACE 4
INTRODUCTORY STUDY 5

QUESTIONS AND NOTES

STUDY 1 – TRACING MISSION IN THE OLD TESTAMENT 7
STUDY 2 – PREPARING AN OLD TESTAMENT MISSIONARY 11
STUDY 3 – THE NEW TESTAMENT CHALLENGE TO MISSION 14
STUDY 4 – HINDRANCES TO MISSIONS 17
STUDY 5 – A MISSIONARY CHURCH – CO-PARTNER IN GOD'S PLAN 21
STUDY 6 – CHURCH AND MISSIONARY = POWERFUL TEAM 25
STUDY 7 – WHAT ABOUT MISSION AND ME? 28
STUDY 8 – BEING EQUIPPED FOR MISSION 32
STUDY 9 – MISSION SERVICE: A MULTI-FACETED MINISTRY TODAY 35
STUDY 10 – MISSION: GOD'S CHALLENGE TO EVERY CHRISTIAN 38

A RESOURCE LIST FROM MISSIONS 41
LEARN MORE ABOUT WEC INTERNATIONAL 42

ANSWER GUIDE

STUDY 1 46
STUDY 2 46
STUDY 3 47
STUDY 4 48
STUDY 5 49
STUDY 6 50
STUDY 7 51
STUDY 8 52
STUDY 9 53
STUDY 10 54

PREFACE
GEARED FOR GROWTH

**'Where there's LIFE there's GROWTH:
Where there's GROWTH there's LIFE.'**

WHY GROW a study group?

Because as we study the Bible and share together we can

- learn to combat loneliness, depression, staleness, frustration, and other problems
- get to understand and love each other
- become responsive to the Holy Spirit's dealing and obedient to God's Word

and that's GROWTH.

How do you GROW a study group?

- Just start by asking a friend to join you and then aim at expanding your group.
- Study the set portions daily (they are brief and easy: no catches).
- Meet once a week to discuss what you find.
- Befriend others, both Christians and non Christians, and work away together

see how it GROWS!

WHEN you GROW ...

This will happen at school, at home, at work, at play, in your youth group, your student fellowship, women's meetings, mid-week meetings, churches and communities,

you'll be REACHING THROUGH TEACHING

INTRODUCTORY STUDY

GETTING TO GRIPS WITH WORLD MISSION

What would you like to be when you grow up Jonathan?'

'A missionary on furlough!'

Jonathan really thought that being a missionary was a piece of cake. What do you think?

Maybe you haven't given much consideration to this issue. Maybe you think missionaries are an extinct species.

What does God say about missions?

This study aims to provide a basic understanding of Christian mission from a Biblical perspective. Our objective is to stimulate interest and participation in the task of reaching a lost world. As you search the Bible text you will find the true facts for yourself.

1. Read *Psalm 119:105; I Corinthians 2:11-12*. What is the source of the knowledge we will gain and how is it made clear to us?
   Joshua 1:8; Psalm 119:97-99. Do we learn by simply reading?

2. Discuss Revelation 13:8b; John 1:29; John 3:16, 17.
   When was the Lamb slain? Who was the Lamb?
   Why did God send His Son into this world?
   In the light of your discussion, how would you describe the heart of God?

3. Did God's plan succeed? Read I John 3:8; Colossians 2:15; Philippians 2:6-11. What resulted from Christ's death and resurrection?

4. What was Christ's last message to His followers before He returned to heaven? See Matthew 28:18-20.
   Discuss what these verses say to us about:
   a) authority
   b) whom we are to disciple
   c) our surety as we do the work

5. When will our task be finished? (Matt. 24:14; Rev. 5:9)
   Why was the Lord's ministry effective? (John 4:34)
   Why was Paul so greatly used? (Acts 20:24)

What does this say about my life style if I am to be productive for God?
Discuss some of the attitudes which must change as I respond to His call.
How did you describe the heart of God?
If the world is to be reached for Christ what kind of hearts do we need?

A. T. Glover, an authority on Christian mission says:

'The divine search of the Creator for His child begins with the first chapter of Genesis and ends with the closing words of Revelation. God Himself is thus seen as the first and greatest missionary, and the whole Bible as the revelation of His successive outreaches into the soul of man.'

These weeks of study ahead are going to be exciting, stimulating and motivating as we watch God's plan for world mission unfold. The missionary mandate has not been rescinded. It will be ongoing till the end of time. 'When the gospel has been communicated to people of every language group (the meaning of Matt. 24:14) the Lord will return as promised.'

Shall we pray now that our hearts will respond fully to what He is saying so that we can be involved vitally in His great plan and be worthy of receiving His 'Well done' (Matt. 25:21).

STUDY 1
TRACING MISSION IN THE OLD TESTAMENT

QUESTIONS

Many individuals down the years have done a sterling task with respect to world mission, yet the church as a whole has not always done too well. Part of the reason can be attributed to ignorance. William Carey, known as the father of modern mission, was 'wet-blanketed' when he aspired to become involved. To some, the Great Commission of Matthew 28:18-20, is the only known reference to the subject of Christian Mission in the Bible. But Mission is what the Bible is all about.

DAY 1 *Genesis 12:1-3*
a) Abraham was father of the Jews, often referred to as God's chosen people. Which part of the promise shows that, in choosing the Jews, God was not disinterested in the rest of the world?
b) What is the blessing promised to all the people of the earth through Abraham and how is it received (Rom. 4:16-17; Gal. 3:6-9)?

DAY 2 *Exodus 19:4-6; 1 Peter 2:9*
a) What missionary role did God give to Israel through Moses?
b) What message did Peter give to the church of his day?

DAY 3 *1 Kings 8:41-43; Isaiah 56:6 and 7*
a) What does Solomon pray for non-Jews who visit the temple?
b) Describe the similarities in Isaiah's declaration.

DAY 4 *Psalm 67*
'The Psalter is one of the greatest missionary books in the world, though seldom seen from that point of view' (Peters 1972). List the ideas here which cause this Psalm to be described as missionary.

QUESTIONS (contd.)

DAY 5 *Isaiah 42:1-8*
How are these verses relevant to mission? Why do you think so? The Old Testament prophets have a distinct missionary emphasis.

DAY 6 *Isaiah 45:22; 49:6; 66:18-23*
Express in your own words the missionary messages found in these verses.

DAY 7 *Habakkuk 2:14; Zechariah 9:9-10*
a) How far reaching and effective will the message be?
b) Will the King return only for Israel?

NOTES

Think of a piece of orchestral music. How often the composer will weave through the whole work, a motif which is the essence of the piece, and which is recognizable from time to time. Perhaps it will be introduced by the violins, picked up later by the oboe, and included in the brass section – but each time we say, 'There it is again!'

In much the same way God emphasizes in His Word, right from the first book, the desire of His heart: that all nations of the earth will be blessed with the message of salvation.

Let's peep into Genesis and see how that 'motif' comes through at some of the most critical times in early history.

* * *

- An old man sits dreaming in the sun. But look! Here are visitors. He greets them, then hurries to his ninety year old wife to urge her to prepare food for them. The guests bring a message: 'About this time next year you and your wife will have a son'.
  And Sarah laughed – who wouldn't?
  Before the visitors leave, the Lord, assuming the birth of the son, reiterates the promise given twenty-five years before:
  'Abraham will become a great nation, and all nations on earth will be blessed through him'.

- Here is the same old man standing on a mountain. In front of him is an altar of stones, and bound to it that promised son, now a grown boy. Abraham takes the knife to kill his son – but God intervenes.
  'Abraham, don't do it! Through this son, your offspring, all nations on earth will be blessed, because you have obeyed Me.'

- Now the boy has become a married man – but what is he doing? The crops have failed and there is famine, so he is packing all his belongings and taking his family south. What a crisis! Where will he go?
  He is heading for Egypt when God calls, 'Stop, Isaac. Stay in Gerar for a while, and I will confirm the oath that I swore to your father Abraham. Through your offspring all nations on earth will be blessed.'

- And who is this young man? He is a fugitive, running from a brother whom he has cheated and who has vowed to kill him. Lonely, frightened and exhausted, he scarcely notices the hardness of his stone pillow before he falls asleep. But the Lord comes to him in a dream. 'I am the Lord, the God of your father Abraham and the God of Isaac. All peoples on earth will be blessed through you and your offspring.'

* * *

In our study this week we have traced the motif through other books of the Old Testament. Can you doubt that God wanted (or still wants) the message of salvation spread to all nations through His chosen people?

We love to quote the beautiful words of Psalm 46:

'Be still, and know that I am God.'

But don't stop there, read on:

'I will be exalted among the nations, I will be exalted in the earth.'

Are you convinced that the Old Testament sets forth the missionary purpose of God? Have you listened to the 'motif' often enough to be able to hum it yourself? And can you sing with David, as they brought home the ark of God: 'Declare His glory among the nations ... Let them say among the nations, "The Lord reigns"!'

STUDY 2
PREPARING AN OLD TESTAMENT MISSIONARY

QUESTIONS

DAY 1 *Jonah 1*
a) How would you describe Jonah as a missionary?
b) Were the sailors Jews or Gentiles?
c) How would you assess their behaviour from verse 16?

DAY 2 *Jonah 2*
a) What would you say is missing in Jonah's prayer?
b) List the characteristics of God you find in this chapter.

DAY 3 *Jonah 3*
a) Despite Jonah's failure, what did God do?
b) How did Jonah respond?
c) Why would you say the message was effective?

DAY 4 *Jonah 4*
a) With whom was Jonah angry and why?
b) How would you describe Jonah's sense of values and attitudes?

DAY 5 *Jonah 1:3; 4:2*
a) How do these verses relate?
b) What was the real reason Jonah didn't want to go to Nineveh?

DAY 6 *Jonah 2:8-9*
a) Discuss this part of Jonah's prayer in the light of chapter 1:3.
b) Read 1 Samuel 15:22; Matthew 26:39. What would you say was basic to sincere prayer?

DAY 7 'And Jonah stalked to his shaded seat and waited for God to come around to his way of thinking. And God is still waiting for a host of Jonahs in their comfortable houses to come around to His way of loving' (Thomas Carlisle).
a) Do you think Carlisle is overstating by using 'a host of Jonahs'?
b) Share some of the insights which have challenged you this week.

NOTES

Why was the book of Jonah written?
> To tell a most unusual incident in one man's life?
> To show that you can't run away from God?
> To provide a graphic story for Sunday Schools?

None of these is the main reason.

As we saw last week, God's overwhelming desire has always been that His message of salvation should be proclaimed by His people to all nations. In the book of Jonah, God showed clearly the main reason why this plan had not succeeded.

God says, 'Go....' Jonah says, 'I won't.'

Why?
Because he is not concerned about the wicked Ninevites, in fact he doesn't want them to be saved, and he cannot tolerate a God who wants to show them mercy.

God said about Israel, 'Here is my servant.... I will make you a light for the Gentiles'.

But Israel was not concerned for the Gentiles, she was so preoccupied with herself that she refused to fit in with God's plan.

God says to His church today, 'Go and make disciples of all nations.' What is our response?

Are we concerned for the other nations?

* * *

How did God deal with this resistance to His will in His chosen servant?

1. He gave Jonah his commission, but did not stop him from going his own way.
2. He blew up a storm – literally. This convicted Jonah of his disobedience, and showed that even Gentile sailors could be saved.
3. He used a great fish as part of His plan to save Nineveh, and to bring Jonah round to His way of thinking.

4. In the fish He showed Jonah that he was in urgent need of saving mercy – the very thing Jonah did not want the people of Nineveh to have.

5. God repeated His order, 'Go to Nineveh.' This time Jonah obeyed, and Nineveh did what Israel had repeatedly failed to do, repented and turned to God.

6. God saw that Jonah's heart had not changed, it was still bitter, still unconcerned for people outside his clique.

7. God tried a last approach, a living, growing visual aid, with an appeal for Jonah to show genuine compassion for the lost.

Did he respond, and have his focus shifted to God's perspective?
We don't know.....

If Jonah is a picture of those who, through bigotry or apathy, have never felt God's heart-beat for mission, then Jesus, the One greater than Jonah, is the exact opposite. Willing, obedient, self-giving and compassionate, He loved the world so much that He gave His life.

So we see that the lessons from the book of Jonah prepare the way for the missionary emphasis of the New Testament – and that will be the topic of our study next week.

STUDY 3
THE NEW TESTAMENT CHALLENGE TO MISSION

QUESTIONS

DAY 1 a) Find the meaning of 'missionary' in the dictionary.
b) What word do you find common to the following references? (Matt. 10:40; Luke 4:18, 43; 10:16; John 3:17; 4:34; 5:24; 8:16; 9:4; 16:5; 20:21; Gal. 4:4; 1 John 4:10)
c) Would you term Jesus a missionary?

DAY 2 *Luke 2:28-35*
a) How do you know Simeon recognized Jesus as a missionary?
b) How would many react to His message?

DAY 3 Put down after each reference what you learn about the importance of mission for the world.
John 1:29 _____
John 3:16 _____
John 3:17 _____
John 4:42 _____
John 8:12 _____
John 17:18 _____

DAY 4 *Refer to yesterday's references and read 1 John 4:14.*
a) List those verses which highlight the Father's role.
b) Which refer to the Son's role?
c) Put into your own words what Jesus means in John 10:16.

DAY 5 *Acts 1:8; 13:1-4; 16:6-7*
What is the Holy Spirit's role in mission?

DAY 6 *Acts 1:8*
a) Find the places mentioned on your Bible map. Why do you think they are mentioned in this order?
b) Which parts of today's world correspond with our Jerusalem, Judea, Samaria and the ends of the earth?

DAY 7 *Romans 10:12-15*
Write down six steps essential to reach a non-Christian for Christ.

NOTES

Clifford Warne, in one of his talks, told this story.

A young angel stood gazing at the galaxies around him, when Heaven's choirmaster happened to come along.

Young angel   What a wonderful sight! Have you ever been out there?
Choirmaster   Yes, we flew to planet earth once to announce the birth of the Creator's Son.
Angel   You mean, the Son of the Creator lived among them?
Choirmaster   Yes.
Angel   Oh, they must be wonderful people.
Choirmaster   Well, they're not. They break His laws deliberately, they assert themselves in defiance of the Creator, and they live their lives as if He doesn't exist.

The young angel was sad.

Angel   Oh, so I suppose He sent His Son to give them what they deserve?
Choirmaster   Well, actually, it was to give them what they didn't deserve – mercy.
Angel   Yes, but the Creator doesn't tolerate rebellion. Rebellion must be punished.
Choirmaster   That's right. It was. His Son took that punishment.
Angel   The Son of the Creator died for the rebels?
Choirmaster   Yes. It's absolutely incredible, isn't it? Although they rebelled, the Creator didn't stop loving them, so He sent His Son on a rescue mission. It was a mission that would cost Him His life's blood as an earthling. He suffered and died, the innocent for the guilty, to bring them safely home to His Father.

* * *

In our study we have seen how this rescue mission was for the whole world, not just for the Jews. As God looks at planet earth, He sees the whole of mankind, and He knows that every person, irrespective of race or colour, has the same need – the need of a Saviour.

* * *

Jesus, in His three-year ministry, demonstrated His love for all people by His attitude to –

a Roman centurian,
a Samaritan woman,
a Samaritan leper,
a Greek woman from Syrian Phoenicia,
a demon-possessed Gadarene man,
and a Canaanite woman from Tyre

His mission was indeed to be a light to the Gentiles. He said, 'When I am lifted up from the earth, I will draw all men unto myself'.

Before He returned to the Father, He gave His disciples this command: 'Go and make disciples of all nations'. Now Jesus had previously told them: 'This gospel of the kingdom will be preached in the whole world as a testimony to all nations, and then the end will come' (Matt. 24:14). Now He assures them: 'I will be with you always, to the very end of the age'. Thus He made it clear that the mission of His church was to be worldwide evangelization until the end of this present Age.

* * *

What happened on the day of Pentecost?

The Holy Spirit gave the disciples power to speak in a variety of non-Jewish languages, reinforcing the fact that He was equipping them to evangelize all nations.

As we read through Acts, we see the Holy Spirit guiding – and sometimes pushing – the believers out to spread the message of salvation to Jerusalem, Judea, Samaria and further afield, so that anyone who called on the name of the Lord would be saved.

STUDY 4
HINDRANCES TO MISSIONS

QUESTIONS

DAY 1 Suppose it is true that those who have never heard the gospel are not lost until they hear and reject it.
a) What effect would this have on world mission?
b) Ephesians 2:3; Romans 3:9, 23. Why are unbelievers lost?

DAY 2 *Romans 1:20*
a) Have the unbelievers lived up to the revelation given in Creation? Which part of this verse is particularly condemning?
b) Romans 1:32; 2:14-15. Have the unsaved lived up to the light of conscience? Discuss your answers.

DAY 3 a) Universalism is a belief that all will be saved in the end. What effect would this have on mission?
b) Matthew 7:13-14; 13:36-43; 25:41; 2 Thessalonians 1:6-10; Revelation 20:15. How do these verses refute this point of view?

DAY 4 a) Another view says there will be a further opportunity to respond to the gospel after death. How would this affect missionary endeavour?
b) Luke 16:19-31. What does this story teach us?
c) Hebrews 9:27. Discuss how this verse makes the same point.

DAY 5 a) 'Young man, sit down. When God decides to convert the heathen He will do so without your help or mine.' This is what was said to William Carey when he aspired to go to India as a missionary. Discuss how this view would cripple missions. (This belief over-emphasizes the sovereignty of God to the neglect of human responsibility.)
b) 1 Corinthians 3:6-9; 2 Corinthians 5:20; Romans 10:14. How could these verses be used to refute this point of view?

QUESTIONS (contd.)

DAY 6 *Deuteronomy 29:29*
What is the secret and what is revealed regarding world evangelization? Mark 13:32-33 and Ephesians 1:9 will help in your discussion.

DAY 7 *Isaiah 42:8; John 14:6; Acts 4:12; 1 Timothy 2:5*
What do these verses say about yet another view, namely that Christianity is only one of many ways to heaven?

NOTES

JIM
My church depends on me to run its street kids' programme. How could I even think of going overseas when so many here need Jesus?
That's a good place to start: help street kids while you can. However, do some honest thinking and ask yourself if the needs aren't greater in other parts of the world!

PATRICK
I've been offered a promotion at work. Prestige brings openings to share Christ with top brass. And there'll be extra cash for needy causes including missionaries.
Witnessing at work, helping the poor – even missionaries! – sound like good reasons to keep your job. But are you quite, quite sure your own security isn't your basic motive? Never forget that God can and will supply all you need as you obey him.

HELEN
My problem is leaving friends and family. I can't bear the thought. They feel upset about it too. In fact they all advise against my interest in missions, afraid my life will be wasted.
Of course you will miss each other. Sacrifice is part of the Christian life. But there will be friendships, letters, home leave and all kinds of communication methods in the future. By the way, have you read Matthew 19:29 lately?

SUE
They say eligible men are scarce on the mission field. Well, I'm single and want to be married. I'd rather stay at home where I'm more likely to find a husband.
It's true. As a missionary you could become one of those wonderful single ladies known as 'the men for the job'. On the other hand, who knows? Mr. Right might happen to be waiting for you out there. Why not trust God to arrange His very best for you?

PHIL
Missionaries have to be well educated, able to study and preach. All I can do is practical work like building and plumbing, so what's the point in applying for a mission field job?
Your skills are desperately needed, and as a man you can relate to men in a society where women must keep their distance.

MIKE AND JENNY
What about our children? Would the Lord ask us to sacrifice their chances of education? Life in the third world would ruin them.
If your call leads you to a country with limited facilities for schooling, take heart from the testimonies of other missionary parents! Living in a foreign land is an education in itself. Schools for Missionary Kids provide good teaching and nurture. Father God loves your children as much as you do, and will never let them down.

KEVIN
At uni we studied a novel telling how 'things fall apart' when Christians bring their western ways to Africa. Converted nationals can be ostracised by their peers. Rather than change their culture, isn't it better to leave them as they are?
Enemies of the gospel will use books, lecture rooms, radio, TV, newspapers, anything, to hinder the spread of Christ's message. In print you will also find accounts of grateful Africans (and others) set free from fear of evil, happy to know their sins are forgiven. The only culture needing change is whatever runs counter to God's beautiful ways.

STUDY 5
A MISSIONARY CHURCH – CO-PARTNER IN GOD'S PLAN

QUESTIONS

DAY 1 *Acts 11:19-30; 13:1-4*
a) What part had Barnabas and Saul played in the church at Antioch?
b) Why would God send his best men away from the church?
c) Discuss the principle involved here for would-be missionaries.

DAY 2 *Acts 13:1-3*
a) Were Barnabas and Saul 'called'? By whom?
b) How did the call come?

DAY 3 *I Corinthians 1:2, 9; I Peter 2:9*
a) In what sense are all Christians called?
b) Discuss the call here compared with that of Acts 13:2

DAY 4 *Acts 13:1-4*
a) How significant is 'praying and fasting'?
b) Write in your own words the message God gives here.

DAY 5 *Acts 13:1-4*
a) Of what advantage was it to Barnabas and Saul that the Holy Spirit had spoken to others about their call?
b) List the advantages to someone in your church sensing God's call if this principle was in operation.

DAY 6 *Mark 5:23; Acts 8:17; 9:17-18*
a) How significant was this 'laying on of hands'?
b) What resulted from doing this?

DAY 7 *Acts 13:3; 19:6; I Timothy 4:14*
What resulted from the 'laying on of hands' in these instances?

NOTES

How did the early missionary churches function? What were their features? What were the faith targets? We are going to put the spotlight on 12 situations that reveal some of the vital principles by which they operated.

1. HEAD DOWN, THEN CHIN UP
The Jerusalem church knew how to pray. Acts 4:23-31 is a good example of Spiritual Warfare. Peter and John were forbidden to spread the good news. So did the church lie down to this edict? No way. They had a prayer meeting instead. Here's what they told the Lord, in modern terms:

   a. 'Now Lord, you're in charge here' (v. 24).
   b. 'You allowed wicked men to kill your Son' (v. 28).
   c. 'We are up against some tough enemies' (v. 29).
   d. 'We are going right ahead with sharing your word' (v. 29).
   e. 'Continue to use us to your glory' (v. 30).

2. LET'S HELP THESE NEW CHRISTIANS!
When the Holy Spirit started to work mightily in Antioch about 500 km away, and there were lots of new converts, the Jerusalem church sent a mature worker – Barnabas – to teach them and give them pastoral care (Acts 11:19-26).

3. LET'S HELP THESE OLD CHRISTIANS!
When a severe famine spread over the Roman empire, the church at Antioch decided to help their brothers and sisters in Jerusalem with some finance which they sent with Barnabas and Saul. The churches in Macedonia also pitched in (Acts 11:27-30; 2 Cor. 8:1-2).

4. WHO, ME LORD?
When the leaders of the Antioch church were praying and fasting they became conscious that the Holy Spirit was asking them for a big sacrifice, namely to release two of their most mature workers for new missionary outreach elsewhere. (Was this the first missionary society?) This incident is fascinating not only for what they did, but for what they DIDN'T do! See Acts 13:1-4.

   a. No mention of a committee meeting to discuss the Spirit's direction!
   b. No mention of a congregational meeting to seek approval.
   c. No mention of finance!
   d. No instructions to the mission group on what they had to do, or where they had to go.
   e. No discussion about the missionaries' suitability.

5. DO IT OUR WAY
The Jerusalem church had a problem. Some people were saying that the new Gentile Christians ought to keep to the rigid Jewish rituals. So they had a conference. The result of this was a clear statement that showed a gracious and loving concern for new Gentile believers everywhere. In effect they said 'We don't want to burden you with our Jewish regulations. Just stay away from food that has been sacrificed to idols, and from loose living' (Acts 15:24-29).

6. HE HADN'T GOT IT RIGHT
The new church at Ephesus welcomed an eloquent evangelist from Alexandria called Apollos. However, they noticed that his message was incomplete – he didn't know about the work of the Holy Spirit. So two of the members took him home for lunch and filled him in!

It is interesting that when later he said he would like to move on to South Greece, the church was enthusiastic about him going, even though he had known the fuller message for only a short time (Acts 18:24-28).

7. NOW HEAR THIS
The elders of the Ephesus church were keen to do their job well, so when an opportunity arose for them to have a leadership seminar under Paul, they jumped at it. Paul made it clear that a leader's responsibility involved maintaining a vision for outreach. Note these statements from chapter 20:

a. 'I have told both Jews and Greeks that they must turn to God in repentance' (v. 21).
b. 'I consider my life worth nothing ... if only I may finish the task ... of testifying to the gospel of God's grace' (v. 24).
c. 'I have not hesitated to proclaim ... the whole will of God' (v. 27).
d. 'Help the weak ... It is more blessed to give than to receive' (v. 35).

8. CASH FLOW
The church at Philippi had a real concern to help missionaries, and sent Paul gifts of money on a regular basis (Phil. 4:10-18). They even sent someone to look after his needs for a while (Phil. 2:25).

9. LET'S GO!
The church at Thessalonica was well known for its missionary outreach (1 Thess. 1:7-8).

10. HANG IN THERE
In letter after letter Paul begged the churches to be much in prayer for his outreach (Rom. 15:30; Eph. 6:18-19; Col. 4:2-3; 2 Thess. 3:1). Paul states his appreciation for the prayers of the church at Corinth (2 Cor. 1:11).
    He, of course, was constantly in prayer for them (Rom. 1:9; Eph. 1:16; Col. 1:3, 9; Phil. 1:4; 1 Thess. 1:2).

11. HELP THE MISSIONARIES ALL YOU CAN
Paul made a point of encouraging churches to look after those who came to them while in full-time ministry.

    a. The Corinthian church,   Timothy (1 Cor. 16:10).
    b. The Corinthian church,   Titus and others (2 Cor. 8:23-24).
    c. The Colossian church,   Mark (Col. 4:10)
    d. The church in Crete,   Zenas and Apollos (Titus 3:13).

He also commended individuals who were doing so.

    a. Priscilla and Aquila (Rom. 16:3-4)
    b. The family of Stephanas (1 Cor. 16:15).
    c. Fortunatus and Achaicus (1 Cor. 16:17).
    d. Philemon (Philem. 7).

12. ADVERSITY AND ADVANCE
It is fascinating to see how reluctant missionaries (people who had to flee from opposition and persecution) were the ones God used to start new churches!
    a. Persecution at Jerusalem/Philip/Church in Samaria (Acts 8:4, 5).
    b. Persecution at Jerusalem/Men from Cyprus and Cyrene/Church at Antioch (Acts 11:19-20).
    c. Opposition in Corinth/Paul and Silas/Church in home of Titius Justus (Acts 18:7).
    d. Opposition in Ephesus/Paul/Discussions in the hall of Tyrannus (Acts 19:9).

STUDY 6
CHURCH AND MISSIONARY = POWERFUL TEAM

QUESTIONS

DAY 1 *Read and re-read Acts 13 and 14 over the next 3 days.*
a) Where did Paul's first missionary tour begin?
b) Where did it end?

DAY 2 a) To whom did Paul and Barnabas report back?
b) What did they emphasize in their report?

DAY 3 a) How long did they remain with the Antioch church?
b) Who were touched by their message as they travelled?

DAY 4 *Acts 15:36–18:22*
a) Where did the second journey begin and end?
b) What motivated Paul to go on this journey?

DAY 5 *Acts 16:1-3*
a) How did Timothy become involved in mission?
b) Does this kind of recruitment work today?

DAY 6 *Compare Acts 14:26-28 with Acts 18:23*
a) Describe how Paul spent his time between missionary journeys.
b) Discuss whether 'modern' missionaries spend their leave in the same manner.

DAY 7 a) List from these chapters (13-18) what you have learned of the relationship between Paul and the Antioch church (13:1-3; 14:26, 27; 15:30, 31).
b) Do you see advantages in missionaries having this relationship with their local church? Why?

NOTES

A SCENARIO
Scene 1
The Annual Church General Meeting had begun. The church had proudly and gladly helped one of their members financially for the last two years as she was a student at a Bible School. After all, she was one of 'theirs'! In fact, the first to train for missionary service. Now she was ready to go overseas. Most assumed the church would go on caring for her. So someone quickly moved that the church keep up the financial support. It was vetoed by the leading elder because she was not planning on going out as a member of the overseas mission of the denomination. So that was that!

A COMEDY OF ERRORS
On the part of the church. No one considered:

- what Scripture had to say about it,
- if the church was in fact unable to fulfil both responsibilities – to the denomination and to this one,
- the fact that the denomination had no work in her target country.

But equally the missionary candidate was at fault:

- in failing to fellowship with the church BEFORE making her decisions.

The sending agency was also at fault in failing to initiate a conference with the church to explain its desire to work in partnership with the church, not apart from it.

Scene 2
40 years later. The same church on the eve of another AGM. But what a difference! A would-be missionary couple had consulted with the church leadership in making plans: in fact the church helped in their choice of a sending body. The mission had consulted at length with the elders and involved them in the decision-making. They knew the agency wasn't 'stealing' their members, but using its expertise to facilitate their movement. So the proposal for the church to support the couple in every way was passed unanimously. But how to go about it? The Annual General Meeting chose a small group to 'brain storm' to come up with practical ideas.
Their findings were:-

1. They realized the need to be a friend to the couple:

> ... by writing to them about what was happening locally; giving them the sports results; enclosing newspaper cuttings and copies of the church bulletin.
> ... by making use of modern communications. Phone them once in a while, or use fax or E-mail
> ... by sending them a cassette every now and then of the church service or of some music. Maybe even a video.
> ... by helping them to adjust to the local scene again when they return home for leave.

2. They acknowledged prayer support to be a vital ingredient in effective missionary work. They knew it would be the constant prayers of friends and supporters – in other words the church – that would sustain the couple. They would ask Andy and Liz to send regular letters so that their praying would be relevant.

3. They accepted financial responsibility. The mission's policy was that each member should trust God to supply all financial needs by the provision of specific personal support. He usually did that through His people. Who were 'His people' in this case but them?

Scene 3
A crowd from the church joining family members and other friends at the airport to wave Andy and Liz goodbye. The couple felt humbled to experience such fellowship: the church members felt privileged to be part of this missionary endeavour: the mission rep. couldn't keep a grin off his face. They were in this TOGETHER.

STUDY 7
WHAT ABOUT MISSION AND ME?

QUESTIONS

DAY 1 *Matthew 9:35-38*
a) In the light of Jesus' example and command what should be our response to world needs?
b) Discuss the connection between Matthew 9:37-38 and 10:5-6.

DAY 2 *Matthew 28:18-20*
a) Give the primary reason for our involvement in world mission.
b) Why does the command involve us and not just the apostles?

DAY 3 What reasons are given in the following references for a lack of response to the missionary call? Luke 9:57-62; Philippians 2:19-21; 2 Timothy 4:10; Acts 1:8.

DAY 4 A pig and chicken were reading a sign on the church notice board. 'Ham and egg breakfast tomorrow. Proceeds to missions.' 'Look, you and I are involved in mission' said the chicken. 'Yes, but with a difference. You are only making a contribution, I have to make a sacrifice' replied the pig. Read 2 Corinthians 8:1-5.
a) Is the Macedonian church in the pig or chicken category?
b) Discuss the meaning of 'grace' in verse 1.

DAY 5 *2 Corinthians 8:1-5*
a) Describe the circumstances of this church.
b) Summarize, in three words, their giving.
c) Put verse 4 into your own words.

DAY 6 *Philippians 4:10-19*
a) What kind of missionary support did Paul receive?
b) List the encouragements to missionary giving found in verses 17-18.
c) Does the promise of verse 19 apply to the senders or receivers? Discuss the lessons to be drawn from this.

QUESTIONS (contd.)

DAY 7 *Ephesians 6:18-20*
  a) What is the significance of the 'ALLS' in verse 18?
  b) Why must we be alert and keep on praying?
  c) What does Paul ask himself?
  d) How then should we pray for our missionaries?

NOTES

STOP!
> God's heart is mission,
> Christ's heart is mission,
> Is my heart mission?

Simon and Clare had been considering their future. Now they had their degrees they could have good jobs, a reasonable income, a home of their own. But something was unsettling them....

Simon: 'Did you notice in our reading today how pointedly God challenged his disciples to get into action and reach non-Christians with the gospel?'

Clare: 'Yes, and He seemed to indicate that just as they were responsible for their contemporaries, successive generations were to do their part.'

Simon: 'The Acts story was really thrilling too. When Jesus empowered them by His Spirit, there was no stopping of them. Why, it says thousands were converted through their witness'.

Clare: 'Maybe God is challenging us to become part of His great plan...'

Simon: 'Let's pray about it and be willing for what He shows us.'

CAUTION!
'Watch out' says Paul. 'The devil tried to hinder me in my calling (1 Thess. 2:18) and he will be determined to dissuade you from this course (1 Pet. 5:8). Beware of his tactics. He will get work mates, well meaning friends, relatives, fellow Christians, even your church seeking to throw spanners in the works. Excuses upon excuses will pile up. He will even have you thinking: 'Me? I am not missionary material; I should do another degree; I will consider mission once I've reached **my** goals.' He tried that too. 'I will ascend to heaven; I will sit enthroned; I will be like the Most High'. But God put paid to his plans (1 John 3:8) and we can rely on Christ's authority as we become His ambassadors.'

So Simon and Clare prayed again: 'Lord, forgive us for our self-centred life style. We want you to be in control. We want our hearts to beat with your heart. We want to fit in wherever you want in your plan to finish the task of world evangelization.'

GO!
How? Where? There are so many needs, so many organisations and missions clamouring for workers....

Simon: 'You know Clare, I'm sure the devil wants to confuse us. I've been thinking about how God wanted Israel so to live for Him that the unsaved around them would come to recognize the true God. Peter says that has to be the quality of our lives too. Do you think, for a time, we should pitch in our lot here, work in the church, witness to our workmates and families and just be vital here where He has placed us?'

That was a good place to start, but God led this couple gently on. They saw how God had worked things out for Abraham, Moses, Gideon, Elisha, Isaiah, Paul, the disciples, Hudson Taylor, C. T. Studd, Jim Elliott, Johnnie Blank. He could do it for them. So they planned ahead for Bible Training and practical experience which would fit them for their missionary work.

PROVISION

Simon: 'Well, that's it Clare – our savings gone and no more pay packets to collect. What if we have made a mistake? But we must take God at His Word. He has promised to meet all our needs – according to His riches. Paul didn't seem to worry. He was content whether God provided little or much. He even went back to tent making on occasion, but he was so busy spreading the gospel he had little time for wage earning.'

Clare: 'And I can't recall that he ever made his need known to the churches. He did spend his time between assignments teaching them and telling of God's work in other areas, so something must have rubbed off ...'

Simon: 'And was he ever excited when such a poor church as the Macedonian one gave spontaneously, joyfully and sacrificially to see his needs met?'

So Simon and Clare prayed yet again ... 'Lord, we believe you mean what you say, that if we push right on and seek to extend your Kingdom, you will supply all our needs. We don't know if you will use individuals, or the church or both to be your channels, but we will rely on your faithfulness.'

* * *

Furlough, eight years later ....
Both the sent ones and the senders rejoice together in God's faithfulness.

'Give, and it will be given ... good measure ... pressed down ... shaken together ... running over' (Luke 6:38).

STUDY 8
BEING EQUIPPED FOR MISSION

QUESTIONS

DAY 1 *Acts 13:2-3; Matthew 28:18-20*
a) Enumerate ways in which a call might be confirmed.
b) To whom is the promise of Matthew 28 specifically given?

DAY 2 *Acts 1:8; Acts 10:19; Acts 6:1-6*
a) Why did Peter witness so effectively? What about us?
b) Describe part of Stephen's equipping. What about us?

DAY 3 *Acts 16:1-3; Acts 4:13; Mark 3:13-19*
a) What was the main part of Timothy's preparation?
b) How did Jesus train his disciples?

DAY 4 *Matthew 8:3, 4; Luke 17:11-19; John 11:4, 45; 12:9-11*
a) What part did miracles of healing play in Jesus' ministry?
b) Do 'modern' missionaries exercise such a ministry and if so what would be possible dangers?

DAY 5 *1 John 3:16*
a) Who is our supreme example of sacrifice?
b) Discuss ways you think missionaries today might have to sacrifice.

DAY 6 *1 Corinthians 12:7-11; Ephesians 4:11-16; 1 Corinthians 13*
a) List Paul's spiritual and natural gifts.
b) In the allegory of the body, how are these gifts to be used?

DAY 7 a) Suppose we are not 'sent' to the mission field, where does our missionary obligation lie?
b) Discuss possible effective areas of ministry where we can be used at home.

NOTES

We have seen throughout these studies that the call to mission is very strong. Yet many people spend their lives waiting for a spectacular and personal 'call'. The whole mission challenge of scripture is encapsulated in Matthew 28:18-20. If you have an urge to get the gospel to unreached peoples, you can be sure God has laid that burden on your heart. You should go straight ahead preparing for His service, knowing He will truly direct you in the line of His will (Prov. 3:5-6).

PREPARATION COVERS FOUR AREAS:
SPIRITUAL: This is the preparation of *HEART* – to love God thus leading to spiritual maturity.

It is absolutely imperative that you develop a strong, intimate fellowship with the Lord. Start right where you are.

a) Daily, vital digging into God's word and a meaningful prayer life.
b) Be available in your local church where your gifts will be recognized and developed.
c) Get involved in outreach, preaching and teaching as much as possible – under the watchful eye of your minister and church leaders.
d) Be involved in praying for missionaries both in your personal prayer times and in mission-hearted prayer groups.
e) This should lead to a change in moral character. Sharpen up areas where you could be weak or actually lacking such as transparency of life, absolute honesty, humility, stick ability (one of the prime essentials for a missionary!) sensibility with finance, sexual purity, compassion, tolerance etc.

ACADEMIC: This is the preparation of the *MIND* – to know God's word, leading to academic excellence. You may not be an academic person, but never be satisfied with the level you have reached just now. Stretch forward for more knowledge of the Bible, of Christian doctrine, of the history of the Christian church and of missions. This may come through:

a) Regular ministry in your local church.
b) Attending Bible conferences and teaching seminars.
c) Studying at a recognized Bible Institute.
d) Reading missionary biographies and familiarize yourself with mission agencies – where they work and possible avenues of service.

PRACTICAL: This is the preparation of the *HANDS* – to work for God, leading to professional competence. There are two principal areas here:

a) Being able to do the work to which God has called you. This may be church planting, bible teaching, literature production or whatever. The important thing is that you develop the gifts God has given you so that you can cope with the missionary situation, whatever it might be. This does not imply however, that you are not always learning more.

b) Recognize and seek to develop natural skills. Get insights into as many practical areas as possible. (You can't always 'ring' a plumber, carpenter or electrician when emergencies arise.

Knowledge of first-aid, home nursing, bookkeeping, gardening, and general administration can be acquired by doing evening school courses.

Look into educational aids if you have children (you may have to 'home-school' them initially.)

Learn to play a musical instrument which can prove very handy when working in a newly developed area.

Correspond with someone from the field of your calling and pick up all the hints and advice you can get as you prepare.

WILLINGNESS: This is the training of the *FEET* – to go where God directs and to stay there until the work is done. The missionary endurance is essential if the job is to be done. Jesus came not just to start the work of redemption but to complete it. He calls us to have the same attitude of seeing the job through to the end.

STUDY 9

MISSION SERVICE:
A MULTI-FACETED MINISTRY TODAY

QUESTIONS

DAY 1 Read this week's notes, section 1, points 1-5. Discuss the possible impacts of the different types of missionary approach today. Which would give the most lasting results?

DAY 2 *Mark 1:35; Luke 6:12; John 17; Romans 12:12; Colossians 4:2*
a) Where would you place prayer in mission work priority?
b) How high up the list was it in Jesus' life and works?

DAY 3 *Acts 15:1, 2, 19, 20, 37-40; 2 Timothy 4:11; Ephesians 6:10-13*
a) How plain-sailing is missionary work (refer to 1 Thess. 2:18!)?
b) How can problems and conflicts be amicably resolved?

DAY 4 *Acts 10:44–11:3; Acts 8:1-5*
a) What kind of spirit showed up in the early church?
b) How does God look on the peoples of the world? (Acts 10:34-36)
c) What means did God use to get the gospel beyond Jerusalem?

DAY 5 *Acts 16:1-4 (1 Timothy 4 and Titus 1:4 and onwards are helpful)*
a) What method did Paul have of training younger workers?
b) What method did he use in reaching many with the gospel? (Think of 2 Cor. 11:26a and refer back to Questions for study 6.)

DAY 6 Read this weeks Notes section 2, points 1-6.
a) Discuss the advantages of witnessing as a family as against a single person on the field. Disadvantages too?
b) What are some of the hurdles a new missionary faces?

DAY 7 Read the Notes section 3, points 1-3.
If a missionary has to leave the field for family or health reasons, is he lost to the missionary cause or can he fill a niche at home?

NOTES

The aim of mission is to see people brought to faith in Christ, built into mature, self-governing churches with missionary vision and outreach. Different means are used to meet these goals.....

SECTION I. *Types of missionaries*
1. *Career missionaries.* These feel God's call to devote their lives unreservedly to missionary work. They go, they learn perhaps more than one language, seek to identify with the people and their culture, plant churches, train leaders, initiate Bible/scripture translations and may or may not be involved in ministries beyond pastoral work, e.g. medical, teaching, agriculture etc.

2. *Short term missionaries.* These people are called to a ministry of 'helps' or temporary replacement of a career missionary and give a limited time to field service. Many such 'get the vision' of returning as a full time career missionary.

3. *Team visits* comprise of a group under the leadership of a pastor or some mature worker who visit a field for a short period. They may be involved in a prayer ministry, evangelistic outreach or offer practical skills e.g. construction of mission houses etc.

4. *Intercessory teams,* again groups going out by pre-arrangement with field personnel and under mature leadership, to purely exercise the ministry of prayer in resistant countries.

5. *Tent Makers.* Very often the only way into a country which is strongly anti Christian is to apply for a secular position and thus supported within that country, live Christ before the people.

SECTION 2. *The Cost*
Jesus illustrated the danger of starting a task and being unable or unwilling to complete it (see Luke 14:28-32). It is possible for a new worker to go out full of enthusiasm, but in the face of difficulties, discouragement sets in and he may eventually return home. Here are some of the issues to be faced:

1. Difficulty learning the language and with cultural adjustment.
2. Unwillingness to defer to authority. Decisions are taken on a fellowship level at field conferences but a new worker still adjusting, may feel his point of view is discountenanced.
3. Relationship problems can occur especially where two single missionaries from different cultures and countries or from different denominational backgrounds are having to work together.
4. Tensions with nationals – it is easy for the missionary to have a con-

descending attitude rather than accept the national as an equal.
5. Unhealthy friendships – even immorality.
6. Losing out on a devotional life through work pressure.

SECTION 3. *Circumstantial problems*
1. Unforeseen difficulties with government departments over such things as visa extensions. This may involve expensive trips out of the country temporarily till the visa is granted.
2. Health can be a real problem. Unfamiliar food, neglect of hygiene, overlooking the taking of preventative medicine.
3. Education problems – To home school your children or not, to avail yourself of boarding school provision, launch into correspondence courses, are all issues to be considered even before your child is of school age. Further down the line – do I take my family home for teenage years and advanced education or what? These are big issues and many missionaries, now at a stage where they are really valuable in the work, can be siphoned off at this point.

STUDY 10
MISSION: GOD'S CHALLENGE TO EVERY CHRISTIAN

QUESTIONS

DAY 1 *Matthew 4:18-22*
a) Discuss the thought that God only selects specially gifted people for overseas service.
b) Assess some missionaries you know regarding their qualities.

DAY 2 *Exodus 2:1-10; 1 Samuel 17:45-50; Mark 15:16-41*
a) How deeply has Bible narrative affected your Christian life?
b) Discuss some incidents from missionary biographies which have helped you and the importance of learning from such books.

DAY 3 *Acts 13:1-3; Acts 15:40-16:1-3*
a) Find a Bible map of Paul's journeys. Where did they take him?
b) Who were some of his fellow missionaries on these trips?
c) How concerned are you about a particular country or certain missionaries?

DAY 4 *Ephesians 6:19-20*
a) How were the Ephesians to pray for Paul?
b) Could the group pray one sentence prayers now about a missionary, his wife, his children, their health, their spiritual life, unity with his fellow-workers, his ministry. Take just one point each.

DAY 5 *Colossians 4:12; 1 Thessalonians 3:10; Colossians 1:9*
a) How did Epaphras pray for the Colossian Christians?
b) Describe Paul's prayer burden for the churches.
c) What could have happened if he hadn't prayed?

QUESTIONS (contd.)

DAY 6 *Philippians 4:14-19*
a) How did the Philippian church express their concern for Paul?
b) What promise were they given in return?

DAY 7 *John 17:6-18*
a) Put into your own words what Jesus prayed for His disciples.
b) Look back at the meaning of 'missionary' on page 10. What is Jesus saying to you and me in verse 18?

NOTES

'Who? Me? A missionary? But I'm not special. I have no university degrees. I'm just a practical, down to earth person.'

Well, that's just great. God is looking for people like you. Don't neglect your education. Be the best for God in that realm too. But God's heart is set on those who see what He means in I Corinthians 1:18-29. WEC's founder said 'Any old turnip for a head will do...' Well, don't take that at face value. He was really endorsing the I Corinthian 1 angle and emphasizing that a willing, obedient heart burning with the love of God for the lost was the prime essential.

Very often a 'call' to missionary service is initiated through involvement such as belonging to a missionary prayer group. One might, for example, be burdened to 'back up' a friend who is serving God as a missionary. In identifying with that missionary, through prayer and giving, the pray-er might himself be influenced for full time service.

Our study this week emphasizes the importance of prayer both for the workers and the work they do. Also, money doesn't 'drop from heaven' but God uses responsive hearts as His channel of supply and assures the giver that God will take care of his needs. Did you note how earnestly and strenuously Epaphras prayed and also how dependent Paul was on the prayers of others?

Read the story in I Samuel 30. David and his men were pursuing the Amalekites who had taken the Israeli women and children captive. Some of David's men, weakened in battle, 'stayed by the stuff' and quite probably prayed for the others. When David returned triumphantly with the rescued families and plenty of loot, a few of his mean-hearted men said:

'Those who didn't go with us should not share in the plunder'.

David replied: 'The share of the man who stayed with the supplies is to be the same as those who went into the battle'.

So, the 'goers' and those who 'back them up' will share equally in the joy of harvest because they have been 'workers together with God'.

The final word from God's Sent One ...

'I pray now for My "sent ones", unity of purpose, obedience to the Father's will, protection from evil, set apartness for the work of the Kingdom. As the Father has sent Me, so send I you ....'

A RESOURCE LIST FROM MISSIONS

1. *Perspectives on the World Christian Movement*, (edited by Ralph D. Winter and Steven C. Horthorne) is highly recommended for anyone seriously interested in mission.

2. A great way to understand God's involvement in the world is by reading autobiographies. Read about Hudson Taylor, C. T. Studd, William Carey and many others who have served cross-culturally to reach the unreached for Jesus.

3. Try reading some of these books and gain valuable insight into mission:

    Give Me This Mountain. Roseveare, Helen; IVP, 1995.
    God's Smuggler. Andrew, Brother; Baker Book House, USA, 1978.
    50 Ways you can Feed a Hungry World. Campolo T. & Aeschliman G.; Kingsway Publications, USA, 1992.
    Better than the Witch Doctor. Cundy, Mary; Monarch Publications, England, 1994.
    Help, my Halo's Slipping. Dinkins, Larry; Overseas Missionary Fellowship, Singapore, 1990.
    Operation World. Johnstone & Mandryk, Paternoster Publishing, 2001.
    Nine Worlds to Win. McClung, Floyd Jr.; Word Publishing, UK, 1989.
    Rough Edges. Taylor, Rhena; Inter-Varsity Press, England, 1978.
    Prepared to Serve. Williams, Derek; Scripture Union, England, 1989.
    The World Christian Starter Kit. Myers, Glenn; OM/WEC, 1993

4. Visit some of the following Mission WEBsites:
    FEBA   www.feba.org.uk
    OM   www.uk.om.org
    SIM   www.sim.org
    WBT   www.wycliffe.org.uk
    YWAM   www.ywam.org

LEARN MORE ABOUT WEC INTERNATIONAL

WEC's PASSION
WEC workers want to see Jesus Christ worshipped by every culture and nation on earth. The heart of WEC's ministry is to establish multiplying churches among unreached people groups.

The need is great! Every 10 seconds, 5 people pass into eternity without even having had ONE OPPORTUNITY to hear that Jesus loves them! Its people like this for which WEC exists.

WEC's WORK FORCE
1,700 long-term workers from 50 nations work in multicultural teams among 90 unreached people groups. Ages vary and so do skills: church planters, evangelists, teachers, youth workers, linguists, doctors, nurses, vocational trainers, IT experts, builders, accountants and many more.

WEC's LIFESTYLE
- Holiness – living Christ-like lives.
- Fellowship – serving the Lord together in the oneness of Christ.
- Faith – trusting God to open closed doors, pull down strongholds and supply every need.
- Sacrifice – willing to step out of 'comfort zones' and risk all for the sake of the gospel.

WEC's CONVICTIONS
- Convinced that prayer is a priority.
- Upholds biblical truth and standards.
- Works in fellowship with local and national churches, and other Christian organizations.
- Accepts each other irrespective of gender, ethnic background or church affiliation.
- Values servant leadership
- Makes no appeal for funds.

WEC's MOTTO
'If Jesus Christ be God and died for me, then no sacrifice can be too great for me to make for Him.' (C. T. Studd)

WEC ON THE CUTTING EDGE
- Establishing vibrant churches, many of which are in restricted access nations.
- Demonstrating the compassion of Christ to children in crisis, drug addicts and through medical work.
- WEB evangelism, radio work and other media ministries.
- Equipping the church for mission through Bible Training Colleges.

WEC's WEB-SITE
Don't miss this exciting experience! Find out more: **www.wec-int.org**

ANSWER GUIDE

The following pages contain an Answer Guide. It is recommended that answers to the questions be attempted before turning to this guide. It is only a guide and the answers given should not be treated as exhaustive.

GUIDE TO INTRODUCTORY STUDY

Work through the five points – this will take almost one hour – and close the session with honest discussion on the changes required in our lives if we are to become effective for God. A good talking point could be 2 Corinthians 5:15.
Here are the key thoughts which should emerge:

1. God's word is truth.
   If we rely on the Holy Spirit He will make it clear to us.
   As well as reading we need to meditate and pray about new truths till they become part of us.

2. God says the Lamb was slain before time began.
   The Lamb is God's son, our Saviour Jesus Christ.
   God so LOVED the world that He sent His son to redeem it from Satan.
   God's heart is mission – His whole desire is to salvage mankind.

3. God's plan was successful.
   Christ's atoning work destroyed the devil's power.
   He disarmed (evil) powers and authority, making of them a public spectacle and triumphing over them.
   As a result, God exalted Christ 'High above all' – see the total quotation in Philippians 2:6-11.

4. Christ's followers were to continue His work of taking the gospel to all peoples.
   a) Since Christ has all authority now we are to operate with that authority. That is what is meant when we pray 'in the name of Jesus'.
   b) Everyone, every people (called ethnic groups today) must hear.
   c) Jesus promises His constant presence as we witness in His name.

5. The task will be complete when all have heard.
   Christ was utterly obedient to His Father's will.
   Paul lived solely for God's purposes and glory.
   Discussion should bring out the necessity of breaking with self-centred living in the interests of the Kingdom.

Mission – please emphasize these points to your group:

Our God is a missionary God.
The Bible is a missionary book.
The gospel is a missionary message.
The church is a missionary institution.
Christ's mandate is a missionary mandate. (John 20:21)

Missionaries are not born – they are made. The making is a tough experience. The process of response to all the word of God challenges us to be and do, is long and difficult. But for those who persevere it is a rewarding experience.

'If you recognize God's call to be a missionary, don't stoop to be a king' (Source unknown).
'God only had one son and He made that son a missionary' (David Livingstone).

The incarnation set in motion God's purpose to reach the world through His missionary son.

The Biblical definition of missionary covers:

Those who have responded to the call of God to a full time ministry of the word and prayer (Acts 6:14).
Those who have crossed geographical and cultural barriers to preach the gospel where Christ is not, or little, known (Rom. 15:20).

But those who witness to the gospel without fulfilling either of the above, are truly missionaries too.
The need today, as in New Testament times, is for an army of fully committed, full time missionaries, backed up by a praying and supportive 'home team' to pull together and see the task accomplished as speedily as possible.

GUIDE TO STUDY 1

Studies 1 and 2 will clearly show that 'mission' is indeed the theme of the Old Testament books.

DAY 1 a) 'I will bless all peoples of the earth through you.'
b) The blessing of 'justification' came to Abraham by faith and likewise 'salvation through faith' will come to all who believe.

DAY 2 a) As God's obedient and holy people they would be a 'Kingdom of priests' i.e. a testimony to other nations.
b) Peter gives the same view, applying it to successive generations of Christians.

DAY 3 a) That they too will come to acknowledge the God of Israel.
b) Foreigners, Gentiles or non Jews who seek to know God will be welcomed to His house and know the joy of the Lord.

DAY 4 As God's ways are made known throughout the nations so His salvation will come to them and all the blessings which accompany it. Contributions will vary, but this is the core.

DAY 5 'In faithfulness He will bring forth justice ... open blind eyes ... free captives....' This whole portion speaks of mission. Verse 6 endorses God's purpose to reach the Gentiles and gives the promise of His enabling as they co-operate with Him.

DAY 6 Personal contributions will vary, but all the references are clear about God's purpose to reach the nations with His salvation.

DAY 7 a) The whole earth will be filled with the knowledge and glory of God!
b) No. His Kingdom will extend to all nations.

GUIDE TO STUDY 2

DAY 1 a) He was a scared, reluctant, disobedient missionary trying to evade God's call.

DAY 2 ... b) The sailors were obviously Gentile men, each crying out to their own gods (v. 5).
c) They wakened up, a bit too late, to the fact that Jonah's God was for real.

DAY 2 a) There is no sign of him repenting for his disobedience.
b) God is prayer hearing (v. 2) faithful (v. 8) the deliverer (v. 6) the holy one (v. 7) bountiful (v. 8) worthy of praise (v. 9) constraining his servant to obedience (v. 9).

DAY 3 a) God re-commissioned Jonah to go to Nineveh.
b) This time he was obedient.
c) Because the people repented on hearing the message (vv. 4,5,6).

DAY 4 a) Jonah became angry with God when He changed His mind about Nineveh's destruction.
b) His reactions reveal self-pity, self centredness and none of God's compassion for a repentant people.

DAY 5 a) The verses have an 'I told you so' attitude showing Jonah's lack of faith in God's wisdom and peevishness at not having his own way.
b) He wanted to get away from God and His call because he didn't feel the people of Nineveh should be spared (4:1-3).

DAY 6 a) It shows a distinct advance in his attitude to God and reveals a growing confidence in God.
b) The basic requirement for answered prayer is to obey the Lord.

DAY 7 a) Christians on the whole are reluctant to follow the Lord's call, especially when it threatens their current life style.
b) There should be many angles for the group to share

GUIDE TO STUDY 3

DAY 1 a) Missionary means 'sent one'.
b) The word common to all is 'sent one'.
c) Jesus was sent from God and is therefore a missionary.

DAY 2 a) He instantly recognized Jesus as 'a light to the Gentiles' (Isa. 42:6).
b) He and His message would be rejected and despised. Isaiah 53:3-4 bears out the prediction of these Luke verses.

DAY 3 The Lamb of God, provided to take away the sins of the world.
God so loved the world that He gave His son....
God sent His son to save the world....
This man really is the Saviour of the world....
I am the light of the world.....
As you sent me into the world I have sent them into the world...

DAY 4 a) John 3:16-17; 17:18; 1 John 4:14.
b) John 1:29; 3:17; 4:42; 8:12; 17:18; 1 John 4:14
c) 'There are people outside the nation of Israel whom I want to win. They will respond to what I say and become part of my flock – I will be their shepherd'.

DAY 5 The Holy Spirit calls out, sets apart, leads, guides and enables those who follow Christ in service.

DAY 6 a) Have a map handy and point out Jerusalem, Judea and Samaria and the 'uttermost parts'. We start witnessing where we are and move on as and if the Lord directs.
b) These vary depending upon the geographical location of groups.

DAY 7 a) Someone has to be SENT (15), the Word PROCLAIMED (14), people must HEAR (14) and BELIEVE (14), by CALLING on the name of the Lord (13-14); He will bless (12).

GUIDE TO STUDY 4

DAY 1 a) Our theological convictions directly influence our attitude to missions. This week we have touched on five mistaken views. If we really believed people are saved without hearing the gospel, we would have little incentive for mission.
b) Unbelievers are lost because, like us, they are sinners and need salvation.

DAY 2   a) No, they have not; they are 'without excuse'. There is evidence of God's power and divine nature all around us.
b) No, they have not. Men everywhere seek to excuse themselves and others (Rom. 1:32) or set up their own standards (2:14) for 'salvation'.

DAY 3   a) If, in the final analysis, all are to be saved, then we can sit at ease where we are and do nothing about mission.
b) These, and many more scriptures, make it very clear that those who are not saved by grace are condemned and worthy only of rejection and hell.

DAY 4   a) We would like to think that God would give a second chance after death to those who reject him now. If this were true there would be no need for missions.
b) There is no second chance (Luke 16:26).
c) For unbelievers there is only judgment and hell after death.

DAY 5   a) An unbalanced view on sovereignty versus human responsibility cripples the missionary thrust.
b) They all indicate that God needs our co-operation in the task i.e. a mouth to communicate the truth.

DAY 6   The truth of the gospel is revealed for us to receive and communicate. The secret things only God knows, e.g., when this day of opportunity will close.

DAY 7   There is only one way. Jesus said 'I am the way...'. Only God can open blinded eyes and He will not share His glory with any false God or idol (Isa. 42:6-8).

GUIDE TO STUDY 5

DAY 1   a) They encouraged the baby church, staying for a year and teaching them the word of God.
b) It is inevitable that God would call out stable, dependable and useful ones for His purposes.
c) Aim at being the 'best for God' in the home church so that the church approves the genuineness of the call.

DAY 2 a) Yes. The Holy Spirit (Acts 13:2b).
b) Through the church leaders as they prayed together.

DAY 3 a) Initially, believers are called into fellowship with His Son, exhorted to be like Him (holy) so that they become witnesses of His grace to unbelievers.
b) The Acts 13 case was to specific men for a special task.

DAY 4 a) When we set aside time with God, refusing interruptions, it gives opportunity for the Holy Spirit to speak to us clearly.
b) 'I have singled out Paul and Barnabas for a special task, so release them from other responsibilities for this ministry.'

DAY 5 a) It must have been very encouraging and confirming that the message was received and relayed by godly, praying men.
b) Such a method practised in our churches today would certainly be reassuring for missionary recruits.

DAY 6 a) This action indicates true identification with the person's call and ministry. It also indicated a dependence on God.
b) There was a very definite work of God done in each instance.

DAY 7 There was instant obedience to the will of God; they were empowered for service; spiritual gifts operated through them.

GUIDE TO STUDY 6

DAY 1 a) Trace Paul's route by locating it on a Bible map.
b) The first journey began and ended at Antioch.

DAY 2 a) To the church at Antioch.
b) There had been much blessing, but especially that the Gentiles were now responding to the gospel.

DAY 3 a) A long time – no stated specific duration.
b) God confirmed His presence with the two men by performing miracles through them (ch. 14:8-10), but many were discipled, converts strengthened (vv. 21, 22) and Gentiles converted (v. 27).

DAY 4 a) The second journey started and ended at Antioch.
b) Jewish legalism, especially the rite of circumcision, was being imposed on the new Gentile converts. The missionaries discussed this issue with leaders in the Jerusalem church who commissioned them to go and correct this error (ch. 15:22-30).

DAY 5 a) Christian leaders approved Timothy's testimony and recommended he accompany Paul.
b) Some churches do this, and there are indications of a growing desire to exercise the method more fully.

DAY 6 a) Paul took a 'busman's holiday' instead of furlough! He went back to his home church and exercised a ministry of encouragement, teaching and sharing results of his tours.
b) Missionaries today see this as valuable, but not all churches welcome it.

DAY 7 a) Paul had good relationships with the church which received him warmly and accepted his ministry.
b) The same should hold for today's missionary as distinct benefits can be reaped by missionary and church through this interaction.

GUIDE TO STUDY 7

DAY 1 a) Surely our response should be to become involved – how can we ask the Lord for workers if we ourselves are not willing?
b) Verse 38 is a general challenge to everyone, verse 5 is a specific injunction to specific people.

DAY 2 a) Because Jesus has commanded us to go!
b) The apostles were there to meet the need of their generation. Successive generations, to the end of time, are to be involved.

DAY 3 Home and family have prior claim; personal plans and ambitions supercede Christ's claims; the 'world' is more attractive than serving Christ; lack of spiritual power.

DAY 4 a) The pig category – willing to sacrifice for the gospel's sake.
b) The grace of God had brought the Macedonian Church much blessing – that same grace motivated them to reach out and bless others.

DAY 5   a) Despite their poverty and obvious struggles as a church they gave even beyond their means.
b) 'Over and above' i.e. they gave spontaneously, generously and joyously.
c) 'They pled with us to be allowed the privilege of helping the missionaries.'

DAY 6   a) Paul's reliance was on the Lord (v. 13) but he graciously received support from the church.
b) Paul saw their giving was primarily 'to the Lord', credited to their spiritual account (Luke 12:33) and amply met his needs – and told them so.
c) The promise is to all who give out of obedient and loving hearts.

DAY 7   a) 'All' indicates a quality of life, an attitude of heart, arising from an intimate walk with God.
b) There is need for constant watchfulness (1 Pet. 5:8) if we are to guard against the devil's attacks.
c) He wants boldness in his witness and clarity as he ministers the word.
d) The very same, for the battle is the same.

GUIDE TO STUDY 8

DAY 1   a) One would sense a burden for a particular area – people group and/or a deep peace as the thought of going and/or there would be concurrence by spiritual leaders and/or most importantly, confirmation from the Bible.
b) The promise is to all who obey Christ's command.

DAY 2   a) He had the equipping of the Holy Spirit – which we need too in our service for Jesus.
b) Stephen just practically served others and that is where we should begin too – with humble and willing hearts.

DAY 3   a) He worked with and learned from more experienced men.
b) By example and encouraging them to witness.

DAY 4   a) Many believed in Christ as a result of healing miracles, but not

all pressed on to deeper faith.
b) Unless solid teaching of God's word accompanies a ministry of healing there is grave danger of misplaced faith and stunted spiritual growth.

DAY 5 a) Jesus paid the supreme price for our salvation....
b) Various answers may be given – leaving behind family and well-paid jobs, steeping off the career 'ladder', limiting opportunities for marriage.... However, no sacrifice on our part can match the sacrifice that Jesus made!

DAY 6 a) Paul seemed to exercise most of the gifts, but outstandingly he had leadership, was an encourager and had clarity in teaching. His natural abilities derived from his education and trade also stood him in good stead.
b) God's gifts are given to be used in love and humility within the 'body' of Christ, His church.

DAY 7 a) We start where He has placed us – in our houses, communities, work places, church.
b) The way could open up for specialized ministry e.g. prisons, hospital visitation, young peoples work and so forth.

GUIDE TO STUDY 9

DAY 1 Valuable contributions can be made at all levels, but for Church planting and growth, the career missionary probably is the most valuable. (In 'closed' countries there may be no other option than to secure employment. However, wonderful opportunities can arise through the Christian worker living a Christ-like life in the 'market place' and bearing witness among one's neighbours.

DAY 2 a) Prayer is absolutely vital to all Christian ministry. Every move forward must be covered in prayer. The missionary who is too busy to pray is too busy. Both private and fellowship prayer are important.
b) Jesus' whole ministry was bathed in prayer.

DAY 3 a) Advance into non Christian territory is always opposed – the devil will do all he can to hinder.

	b) Difficulties can and will be overcome through prayer, consultation with leadership, heart to heart communication and a humble, forgiving spirit.
DAY 4	a) Nationalistic. Jews found it difficult to accept converted Gentiles who would not adhere to Jewish law. Paul and Barnabas were used to convince them otherwise. b) God accepts everyone on equal terms. c) As the result of persecution the Jerusalem church was scattered and so the gospel spread.
DAY 5	a) Paul taught by his own example and literally pushed new workers into action but kept guiding and helping them. b) Paul moved from city to city, established churches who in turn reached out to the areas around them.
DAY 6	a) A Christian family can be a strong witness in an unbelieving community – have an influence on the growing church by exemplifying love, discipline, respect and regard for others in family conduct. Good teamship between husband and wife, willingness to 'release' each other to areas of service – all are important. In certain cultures 'single witness' men to men, women to women, is absolutely imperative. b) See Notes, Section 2.
DAY 7	With training, field experience and a heart still burning for mission, a returned missionary can be a valuable asset. Areas of opportunity such as prayer, representing a mission, joining mission home staff, educating young people in mission and just being a 'missionary presence' in his or her home church are some of the possibilities.

GUIDE TO STUDY 10

DAY 1	a) All who are saved by His grace and indwelt by His Spirit, irrespective of natural gifts and equipping 'quality' to be His 'sent ones'. Peter, a rough fisherman, filled with God's spirit saw 3,000 brought to Christ at Pentecost (Acts 2:41). b) Personal.

DAY 2 a) Personal. Graphic Bible stories shared even at Kindergarten/ Sunday School level can eventually contribute to our conversion and effectiveness for Christ.
b) Biographies of servants of God can likewise stimulate and motivate us as we see what God does through ordinary men and women.

DAY 3 a) Paul reached out across the then known world, conscious of God's directive and burdened for those who were not Jews (Acts 9:15).
b) Barnabas, Silas, Timothy were some of his fellow-workers.
c) Personal. A heart concern for untouched areas and those concerned to reach them should involve us in reading about them, praying for them, giving to them and going as God directs.

DAY 4 a) That as he preached he might do so with such clarity and fearfulness that the word would be effective.
b) Encourage individuals to take up one point and pray simple, practical, brief prayers.

DAY 5 a) 'Wrestling' indicates intense, strenuous, battling in prayer.
b) Paul prayed CONSTANTLY for the new churches.
c) It would have been easy for these new converts to be led into error and perhaps the gospel plus other pagan or legalistic angles (Acts 15:1, 20).

DAY 6 a) They gave, without any prompting, to support him in his ministry.
b) God is no man's debtor; He meets abundantly the needs of those who give to Him.

DAY 7 a) He prayed for God's continual protection on them, that they might evidence complete unity, be one with the Father's will, that they would be protected from evil (the evil one) and made holy through God's word – set apart for God.
b) Just as Jesus was sent from God for a specific task, so we are His 'sent ones' to reach a lost world.

THE WORD WORLDWIDE

We first heard of WORD WORLDWIDE over 20 years ago when Marie Dinnen, its founder, shared excitedly about the wonderful way ministry to one needy woman had exploded to touch many lives. It was great to see the Word of God being made central in the lives of thousands of men and women, then to witness the life-changing results of them applying the Word to their circumstances. Over the years the vision for WORD WORLDWIDE has not dimmed in the hearts of those who are involved in this ministry. God is still at work through His Word and in today's self-seeking society, the Word is even more relevant to those who desire true meaning and purpose in life. WORD WORLDWIDE is a ministry of WEC International, an interdenominational missionary society, whose sole purpose is to see Christ known, loved and worshipped by all, particularly those who have yet to hear of His wonderful name. This ministry is a vital part of our work and we warmly recommend the WORD WORLDWIDE 'Geared for Growth' Bible studies to you. We know that as you study His Word you will be enriched in your personal walk with Christ. It is our hope that as you are blessed through these studies, you will find opportunities to help others discover a personal relationship with Jesus. As a mission we would encourage you to work with us to make Christ known to the ends of the earth.

Stewart and Jean Moulds – British Directors, **WEC International.**

A full list of over 50 'Geared for Growth' studies can be obtained from:

ENGLAND   *North East/South*: John and Ann Edwards
5 Louvaine Terrace, Hetton-le-Hole, Tyne & Wear, DH5 9PP
Tel. 0191 5262803 Email: rhysjohn.edwards@virgin.net
North West/Midlands: Anne Jenkins
2 Windermere Road, Carnforth, Lancs., LA5 9AR
Tel. 01524 734797 Email: anne@jenkins.abelgratis.com
West: Pam Riches Tel. 01594 834241

IRELAND   Steffney Preston
33 Harcourts Hill, Portadown, Craigavon, N. Ireland, BT62 3RE
Tel. 028 3833 7844 Email: sa.preston@talk21.com

SCOTLAND   Margaret Halliday
10 Douglas Drive, Newton Mearns, Glasgow, G77 6HR
Tel. 0141 639 8695 Email: mhalliday@onetel.net.uk

WALES   William and Eirian Edwards
Penlan Uchaf, Carmarthen Road, Kidwelly, Carms., SA17 5AF
Tel. 01554 890423 Email: penlanuchaf@fwi.co.uk

UK CO-ORDINATOR
Anne Jenkins
2 Windermere Road, Carnforth, Lancs., LA5 9AR
Tel. 01524 734797 Email: anne@jenkins.abelgratis.com

UK Website: www.wordworldwide.org.uk